Jennifer Laughl

Come Walk
WITH ME

Published by Tate Publishing & Enterprises, LLC
127 E. Trade Center Terrace | Mustang, Oklahoma 73064 USA
1.888.361.9473 | www.tatepublishing.com

Tate Publishing is committed to excellence in the publishing industry. The company reflects the philosophy established by the founders, based on Psalm 68:11,
"The Lord gave the word and great was the company of those who published it."

Published in the United States of America

ISBN: 978-1-68207-046-8
Biography & Autobiography / General
16.01.29

Get ready to take a walk with author and life coach, Jennifer Laughlin Stevenson, as she takes you on a journey of determination and perseverance, as you experience her passion for life and for others as she keeps fighting for a life change. Her resilience is inspiring. Sometimes you just have to paint your own doors in life!

This book is dedicated to my parents and siblings for their unconditional love for me; they have always been my biggest fans. There have also been some very influential people in my life that have helped me along the way. Thank you all for your blessings.

To my dear friend Sarah. Thank you for always helping the words hit the paper correctly and always being there when I need you. You are my superhero.

To all my readers, I hope you gain understanding that regardless what happens in life, it's what you do about it that defines us, and every moment is a new chance to change.

Never give up on your dreams; there is always a way.

COME TAKE A WALK WITH ME.

You know, looking back, I am thankful for all the hard times. Not because they were hard of course, but because of what I have been able to do with all those experiences today. I guess the best way to understand is for me start at the beginning of what I remember.

You see, I am the youngest of five children. My mother could have been a beauty queen, and my father was that one guy…you know, the one who was always the best at whatever he did. The quarterback, the track star, oh, and he was handsome and even went to the Olympic trials for diving.

You know, when my father was a boy, he was probably headed to prison, but a man at the swimming pool noticed a talent within my dad and started coaching him. He took the time and redirected my father's energy; it's really an amazing story in itself. My father's home was filled with addiction, violence, and if he wanted to see his parents, he would have to stop by down at the bar. Now my mother, I know she grew up very poor, and I guess she never really shared with me how life was at home other than how she was excited when they got indoor plumbing. However, by the time I came around, I loved spending time with my mom's father. His arms where so large, and he would always be in his spot in front of the TV when I would ride my bike to see him. I would just run down the steps and cuddle up. He never asked me about what was going on at home and just spent time with me. They called him Big Bob. Grandpa had cancer, so the grandfather I knew was much different than what my siblings had a chance to experience. My grandma, well, she doesn't care who you were; you could not get out of there without her feeding you.

My parents got married very young. Mom was sixteen and Dad eighteen. My mom had my oldest sister when she was just sixteen. Now I came much later in life, so I feel I had different parents than my siblings did. I was the oopsie; my mom had her tubes tied then had me. I guess I was meant to be here.

☘ ☘

Let's go this way now...

Now growing up with two brothers and two sisters, well, let's just say it was exciting. Okay, really, it was chaos. Now don't get me wrong; we all loved each other in our own ways, and God forbid you cross one of them if you were not family. It would be war, but when it came to each other, it was no-holds-barred. When they were not trying to kill each other, they had fun scaring each other or pulling pranks on each other, which usually sent them back to fighting.

I can't believe my siblings didn't kill each other, and at times, I felt the same way about my parents. But the one thing I can say when it came to me, they were all so different.

Now I am sure if you spoke to my parents or siblings, you would hear a different perspective on all this, but this is my part of the story and things that are part of my own evolution as a person.

I really don't remember much before I was five years old, but I can say my oldest sister was like a stranger, and she was so mean to my other sister, who I called Sissy, and the oldest of my brothers, who I called Bubba.

꙳ ꙳

Let's sit here a moment…

You know, telling you now, I don't remember feeling scared at all during the chaos. I was just in my own world, I think. There was this one time where my oldest sister was throwing knives at my sissy and bubba, and I was just playing under the coffee table. I should have been screaming and crying, but I just kept playing like it was no big deal.

Now my parents were starting their own business at the time, so they weren't home much, and my sissy was like my mom to me. Oh, she was my world. She would take me on walks to the local candy shop or to the bus stop so we could go to the mall. I loved to look at clothes and get cheap jewelry. She always got me something. She would draw with me and go out and play. Now I have to add something funny here. Let's walk again.

※ ※

Now my parents and siblings would always tell me not to talk to strangers, that I was cute, and someone might want to kidnap me. Oh, this scared me. I knew where all those Blue Star homes were on my route to school. As you will learn, I was, and still am, very literal. So with that said, my sissy dropped me off at school. I remember it so well. I had my canned good I was so excited to give to help someone in need in my hand as I waved good-bye to her with the other. I run up to school, the doors are locked, then I notice nobody was there. So I started the long walk home, but as cars passed, I started to scare myself. I was never to walk alone or this far by myself. Then I remembered I was cute and, well, someone might want to steal me, so I did some problem solving at age five. I thought if I was ugly, nobody would want to steal me, so I made funny faces and walked funny, thinking that would make me look ugly. Okay, so could you imagine seeing this little girl walking down the sidewalk that probably looked like I was having a seizure? But I remember some cars would slow down, and I would panic and do whatever I was doing to a higher level because I thought they wanted to steal me. I did this all the way home.

No, I would do anything to cover for my sissy. She was always running away. I missed her so much every time she left, but I would try to help her. I remember one time I locked the door and shut the window the best I could after she jumped out of it. Dad told me to open that door, and nope, I wasn't going to do it. Well, I learned a door wasn't going stop my dad that day. He wasn't happy. This time she never came back. Well in time she did, but she never lived with us again. It was never the same. After sissy left, I turned into the biggest daddy's girl ever.

Now my bubba would test my dad. Geez, those two went rounds. I never really knew why; it's just how it was. I do remember finding out that some men beat my brother horribly in back of the house we lived in. I saw all the blood on the house, and he looked horrible. Just think, this happened while I was sleeping. My bubba was my funny man; he always made me laugh. We would play silly games, and he would make funny noises. I remember one time he got very serious with me. He told me, "Now you know, JJ (that's what they called me), it's up to you to make Mom and Dad proud as you're the chosen one," then he got all silly again. Well, sometime later, I had to go with my parents to a prison to see my bubba. I loved to go see him. He was my silly bubba. He would write to me and draw me pictures of Garfield. You see, he got involved in drugs and did some bad things, but to me, he was just my bubba. I wasn't scared of the other people in the room. I guess I should have been scared of the whole experience. I knew my bubba did something bad, but I loved him just same, so I thought these other guys could not be that bad because my bubba wasn't.

Now I am jumping around a little, but let me go back to my sissy for a moment. She did finally come back like I said, but she never lived with us again. She got married and had a baby when I was just seven. Whenever she came to visit, or the few times I got to spend the night at her house, I would hold on to her legs so tightly she had to fight me off her to leave. That was so hard for me. My sissy also got into drugs, was in a biker gang, and she danced. I loved to dance, I danced down halls, I danced everywhere. I was in my own little world, but she danced differently than me, but I was sure she was beautiful at it. I remember she went to jail for a while at one point. You know, I don't think I ever went to see her, not sure I even wrote to her. Oh, but I loved her. I'm not sure why. I think she was far away.

I knew at a young age that I never wanted to do drugs. Sometimes I didn't like how my bubba and sissy acted, but I loved them anyway, but I hated drugs because it took them away from me.

🌿 🌿

After Sissy left, remember I told you I became the biggest daddy's girl. Well, I didn't want to be home with my other brother or my mom much, so I was daddy's bat girl for his softball team. Anywhere I could go with him I did.

I mentioned my parents started their own business. Well, here's something right out of the movies for you: they started a private detective and security business. So my time with daddy was going on stakeouts, helping him get people's trash, learning how to size up a room, always knowing how many exits there are and where. My favorite was watching people's body language to see if it matched what they were doing and saying. Again, I thought all this was normal. Didn't everyone do this?

I have no clue what I did to keep myself busy because sometimes it was so boring. One time, my mother and I dropped my father off at a location. He took his camera and headed off into the cornfield. Mom got in the driver's seat and was reading. The next thing I knew, the back doors come flying open, my dad jumps in, and says, "Drive, Carol, drive!" I look past my dad and a dog was hot on his trail. I just laughed, like, yep, fun times with Mom and Dad.

🌿 🌿

I started figure skating and fell in love with the sport. I felt so free on the ice. It was another world for me. Everything stops at the rink doors, and inside, I was me, ice, the music, and freedom. Now I'm sure I wasn't the most technical skater, but I was the most captivating. On the ice, others wanted to be like me, but in the classroom, I wanted to be like everyone else. On the ice, oh, I would feel the music and just move around the ice. Every show I had had a standing ovation and usually got the best of show. Ice skating was my escape from life.

At every performance, my sissy and other siblings would make it a point to watch if they were in town. I have to laugh thinking about this. In the audience, I had my family section. My sissy would bring her biker friends to cheer me on, then I also had a group of teachers right next to them. Very different worlds, but both full of people who were there for me. It went on during high school graduation and college graduation, and I would not have it any other way.

My other brother, he is six years older than me, but I was told he wasn't too happy about my arrival into the family. My mom said he liked being the baby. He wasn't very nice to me, and well, I'm sure I was annoying. I never left him alone, but then I would tattle on him horribly. He was mean. He shoved me in the closet and under my bed. He tied my hair to the banister so I could not follow him around the house when he was watching me. But still I adored him. He was like Dad; he was very handsome, and all his girlfriends took the time to hang out with me when they were around. He played hockey, and like Dad, he was very good. He even played for the local pro team. That was pretty big around here. I know he was proud of me and my skating. I loved to name drop that he was my brother. He was quiet, and well, I demanded attention.

As a young adult, he was teaching Tae Kwon Do at the local gym. I joined the gym to take his class. He's amazing at the sport. I, however, wasn't blessed with his reflexes, so as a child, he could hit (well, tap) me fifty times before I finally got one in on him. So you can see how this might go for me. So yep, I paid a gym membership to have my brother beat me up, something I got at home for free. But I think he enjoyed teaching me. Sometimes he hit me hard and laughed at me. *Jenni, why on earth did you just walk into that one?* He seemed to move at the speed of light. But really this was my favorite time with him, I still don't see him much.

Now back to my mom. I never really gave her much of chance. I wanted her when I didn't feel well; she cooked and snuggled up until I felt better, but I guess looking at this now, my mom was very unhappy. I remember just recently my father telling me how fun and funny my mom was. I never knew she was like that. She was working the family business or in bed with migraine or she would be bashing my dad. Now these two love each other, don't get me wrong, but looking at them, I guess the mom I had was during a time in her life when she was just pissed off. You know, I never have asked my mom if she ever had dreams of her own; I guess I should. She would always tell me how horrible my father was, that I was just like him, and how she always wanted me to do something with my life and not to depend on a man. Okay, now I know as an adult what she meant. I was like my dad in good ways, but then she didn't speak well of him, so I, in my literal-minded, childlike way, thought that she thought I was bad person, so I never gave her chance. When I was little, my dad would try to sit next to my mom, and every time, I would go jump in between them. I didn't want her next to him. My mom was beautiful. I remember just watching her, thinking someday I hope to look like my mom. She and I did spend time together. I'm sure she wished it would have been more, but I did want to learn to cook or sit and read with her, and we loved to watch Disney movies together.

Now I was a very independent girl. They told me I would always yell at them if they tried to help by saying, "I'll do it myself." Sometimes, I think I even parented myself. I was the one that always tried to make everyone happy or get them stop fighting when I got older. I still find things I drew on from when I was little. I drew on everything and on walls, whatever I could find. I never got in trouble. They all just told me whatever I did was beautiful.

You see, in school, I was sent to a special classroom. I was diagnosed with dyslexia. However, I was very social, had lots of friends. At my twentieth year class reunion, a friend had found out about my learning disability and said, "Jenni, I thought you were always going to the smart kids' class." I learned at a young age that your attitude can change the perception of what's truly going on.

Other than on the ice, I really didn't allow myself to feel much emotion. I think this is because I made peace keeper my role in the family. I remember getting so mad on the inside, but smiling at my parents on the outside. I went to a meeting with my parents with teachers. Now the adults spoke like I wasn't sitting right there! The teacher, now this is how I took what she said. Nobody explained anything to me. She said graduating from high school might likely be my highest educational achievement. My dad was outraged. I remember him telling her I could be anything I wanted to be and that the problem wasn't me but them, and we left.

Everything changed from this moment on for me. I don't know what kind of talks the family had about this, but until now did I realize that everyone loved everything I did—the wall drawing were the most beautiful things they have ever seen, all of them, even my brother that didn't like me so much would say, "Looks good, brat." I think my siblings wanted to help me or maybe have chance at life they never felt like they had, and my parents came together when it came to me. Now as a child, I didn't realize it, but it's pretty beautiful and powerful.

That moment at the conference upset me so much that I have spent the rest of my life proving that teacher wrong. Now looking back at this, maybe she didn't mean it that way, but it gave me a fire. Later, I had very supportive special needs teachers that thought more like my parents. Everything changed. I'm sure my parents handpicked my teachers for me from that moment on. Before this happened, I was in a classroom with children with behavioral issues and other learning disabilities. I didn't act out. I just remember sitting there, just wanting to go home, that chaos was my comfort.

I had some special teachers that supported me through everything in school and always made my ice skating shows; and today, one of them is still one of my biggest cheerleaders.

In high school, I was very driven. I was going to graduate early. I was headed to Colorado after graduation to go to a training camp for figure skating, or I wanted to go to the air force academy.

Now my parents found success. Their business was thriving and for a time we stopped moving all the time. See, looking back, my parents did not invest in buying a house or for their future, not something you're taught growing up in poverty. So instead, we took trip to go skiing in Colorado, or sent my brother to training camps for his hockey as he was headed pro, and my bubba and his wife went to live with him in Colorado for summer. You see, my bubba had some pretty bad luck after he got out of prison. I was in junior high when he got a job, and on his way to work, he had a horrible accent. He died a few times, but the efforts of emergency services saved him. He had a head injury, and his legs will never be the same.

Things have never been the same for him, but I love it when he is my bubba.

※ ※

Let's go this way now...

Things changed forever the summer before my junior year of high school. My parents lost everything. We had nothing but a little shack they had just happened to buy off in the country in a really run-down area. So we moved. I saw the light leave my father's eyes; his spark was gone. My mom would go back and forth from hot and cold behavior. So me not wanting to upset them, I never brought up how badly I wanted senior pictures like everyone else and made the best out of what I had. I used to love to go buy clothes, but I learned that material things really didn't matter.

Now to this small town we moved to, there was boy there I dated once when I first started high school. He bought me flowers, and I dumped him. He scared the heck out of me. You see, I had never really let anyone to close to me. I had lots of friends. I was friends with everyone but never let too many get too close. When I did, I would separate myself from them and move to another group of friends. I still struggle with this, but I'm working on letting people in.

Well, back to that boy who is now young man, he adored me and was more than eager to take care of me. He had his own place and a job. I thought if I went with him, that would help my parents as they didn't have to worry about caring for me.

I had no idea what love was. My parents told me as much as I moved out when I was seventeen. They were right, of course. They were worried I was throwing everything away I had worked so hard for, but I was so worried about being a burden to them that I needed to go. Well, not long after that I was pregnant and had a miscarriage then didn't learn anything from that experience and was pregnant again and dropped out of school for the first semester of my senior year.

I got my stuff back together and graduated with my class, graduated from high school, got married, had a baby, and started college all in six months of each other. College was too overwhelming for me at first, so I dropped out and got a job at a local hospital being a housekeeper.

※ ※

Let's go back to that little girl I had. She saved me and my parents, but that marriage was toxic.

I approached the whole pregnancy with a less-is-more attitude, as I was scared to death. My parents never stopped coming over as they watched Kaylee, and we lived with them from time to time as things were a struggle. I didn't do pregnancy well and needed my parents; they had a sense of purpose again.

During childbirth, they told me that they were going to have to use forceps to help get the baby out. I just smiled and said okay, but then…the nurse came at me with these huge metal things. My eyes must have showed my emotions as the nurse said, "Oh honey, these are just to hold the sheet down on your legs." I closed my eyes from that point on and didn't open them until they told me to take a look at my little girl. On my nineteenth birthday, I gave birth to my own miracle. I watched as my parents rushed in to see if we were both okay. My dad asked, "Did you do okay, honey," as he made a right turn for the baby just on the other side of the room. I watched the two of them over my mom's shoulder as she was holding my hand. I watched her little fingers wrap around his finger. I thought to myself, *Well, he is a goner*, just taken out by a ten-minute-old baby as I saw the biggest simile on my dad's face—one I haven't seen in a long time.

After she was born, I was shocked as I gained a lot of weight. Yep, ladies, you can't just eat and eat because you're pregnant; that little six-pound thing left sixty pounds on me when it was all said and done.

Now my parents watched Kaylee when I went back to work, but they still came over daily until then. I remember my dad called to say he and mom were on their way. He heard Kaylee crying in the background. He said, "What's wrong with the baby?"

I said, "She's hungry, and we have to wait twenty more minutes before I could feed her." He told me they would be right there.

Well, he made it in record time, flung that door open, and said, "Jenni, give me that baby," and told my mom to go make a bottle. Now I told my dad that the doctor and nurse said she should eat every two hours. Now I took the doctor's and nurse's words as God telling me himself what I needed to do. My mother explained to me that those words are guidelines, not the law. You see, I'm very literal at times. Yeah, I'm still working on that.

※ ※

My daughter got sick and was in the hospital around her first Christmas. This same time a year ago, my nephew died of SIDS, and he was also born on my birthday a year before my daughter. My brother was at the hospital daily after she was born, as well as every day she was in the hospital just to rock her and let me sleep. *Oh, he does love her*, I would say to myself as I watch him rock her, but he was sure to call me brat when he left, but it was in his own loving way. That was such hard thing to go through but we were all so helpless in how to help him and his wife. Other than the hospital stays, I didn't see him much again.

Now when I was working at the hospital, I wasn't scared to talk to anyone, so I made friends with the doctors and nurses. They keep telling me to go to school, that I should do more with my life than just being a housekeeper; not that that's bad, but inside, I wanted so much more with my life. I still had dreams and goals I wanted to achieve, so I took their advice, headed back to school to be an emergency medical technician, and volunteered as a firefighter. During this time and for years to come, I was going back and forth on welfare and off welfare, trying so hard to make something of myself.

Now after having another child and trying to go back to school again and join the National Guard for a short time, I left that toxic marriage, and I was going to do something with my life now!

☙ ❧

Let's take this path now.

Now I am living with my parents again with two children and attending community college so I can later transfer to the local university. I met a young man that had fun with my kids and didn't tell me I could do this or that. It was like, "Heck ya, you can go to college. You can achieve anything you want," rather than being in a marriage I was just in. Well, three months later, I was married again. Yes, I know! We both got a place in college, but it didn't take long for me to become pregnant, and he was leaving for the service and moved me back with my parents. Again, I don't do pregnancy well, and I had to drop out of school and got stuck in bed, so I just lay in my room and would take one walk to the mailbox every day to see if I had a letter or to mail one off. My kids would come lie in bed with me for a while and would always check on me, but mostly, I watched them play outside in the garden or the wood shop with their grandparents from my window.

When my husband returned from service and having the baby five weeks early, I found myself back in school when the baby was just two weeks old. I was so determined to get this thing done. Now back on welfare for what I promised would be the last time. Living in a married-student housing at the University of Northern Iowa, I felt so close to getting my four-year degree. I spent my time at school working so hard, asking help from some amazing professors that worked so hard with me. They believed in me and my abilities. I was discovering and researching my own disability, figuring out how my brain worked, and once I did, I took off. The university even flew me to Washington, DC, and California to present my research at conferences. Wow, it was amazing. However, life was about to change forever once again.

⚞ ⚟

Let's take this path through the woods now if you don't mind. Will you take my hand as we walk please?

My cell phone would not stop ringing while I was proctoring an exam. Once the last student left, I returned the call. It was the hospital in Charles City telling me my husband was in a terrible accident. I rushed off. He had an angel on his shoulder that day for sure. Nothing was broken on the outside, but when I went by the crash site, he should have been dead; it was horrible. He ended up with a brain injury.

So I went into caretaker mode as I continued school and caring for the children. My brother, remember, had a brain injury, and I was working in medical field long enough to understand what I could be in for. I did what I did best and researched the best way to help. I needed to get those neurons firing again, making new connections. I didn't sleep much during this time in my life. There was so much going on, but I was not going to give up.

However, even though he didn't die that day, my husband left me, but it took me years before I figured that out. I did graduate from UNI, and I started working at a helping agency. Here is a weird twist in my life: my career skyrocketed, but my home life was crumbling, and I was in denial for years. Within six months at my new job and was promoted within the first year, I was then the manager of the service line. The helping profession was a perfect fit. My life experience, my education, and my life passion were all wrapped up into one. Helping children and families in need to find the resources they need to be successful was such a blessing. I also helped develop crisis programs. Not many people could handle that line of work, but remember, chaos is comfortable to me, so being able to help others was very rewarding. Plus, I had such talented staff that made everything work well.

But back at home, my oldest son left me. Looking back at eight, he was pretty smart, and well, he didn't leave me, but he no longer wanted to live seeing me treated the way I was being treated—or him for that matter. Then years later, after my daughter turned sixteen, she too had enough and left. As for me, I was still holding on, thinking it would get better. I didn't want another failed marriage. The husband was back to work now and doing better at work it seems, but at home, there was so much resentment for each other. You see, he became a monster to us during his recovery. The man I married, I did not see him anymore, but he looked like him. Unlike a broken something, you can see that injury, but he looked fine, but he really wasn't. He doesn't remember, and calls the entire event a haze; it was horrible. He found notes he had written, his handwriting was even different and didn't want to believe he wrote them for example.

Life took another horrible turn when one night, his friend from college stayed with us, and they decided to drink and play games like their college days. Know that I don't drink, and I had my youngest at home. Well, let's just say he took what he wanted from me. There was no help as my husband lay passed out and unable to respond to me and scared me. What might happen if my son would wake up? It still feels as though I spent the night with the devil himself that night. We'll just leave that there.

Now some time before that happened, my husband told me that he knows he should love me, but he didn't. He wants to but can't. Forgive my language, but to him, he said I was the bitch that made him get out of that chair. My world came crashing in on me. I didn't leave when things where hard. I stood by him, helped him, and all for what? He hated me, two of my kids left, I'm having my own health problems and a rape to deal with. He just told me he wasn't like me and could not help me the way I needed him to.

Now I am sinking fast. I changed jobs and then left the new one almost a year in because of some issues with the industry I worked in. I started to launch my consulting agency for helping business, and I hit rock bottom—first time I ever allowed myself to fall in my entire life, so you could imagine how dark this time was.

I told my husband I was leaving a year after the rape. The day I told my family I was leaving, my father, mother, and daughter had me moved into my new home before I got done with work.

※ ※

Do you mind if we go this way? The path looks pretty a ways up.

I had another heart procedure looming. In my new place, self-employed with a part time job as well and starting over, but being all alone was the hardest thing. My daughter and son were around a lot more, and well, I think I checked out and just went through the motions of life for a while. Then as I was lying in bed on the day after my heart procedure and tired of being with myself, I noticed the birds singing; it was strange. I know how birds singing could be strange. I realized I had tuned out Mother Nature. I had forgotten to live because I was so focused on surviving.

I gave it all to God that morning. Feeling sorry for myself wasn't anything I had done before, so I moved on.

My parents have been around a lot more again; that was wonderful. My children were over all the time, my consulting was at an all-time high with clients, and I am working on my health. I realized that life wasn't about work. Would my children want a gold plate of my résumé when I was gone, or would they rather want time with me?

Oh, that reminds me, when I first started having heart trouble, I had this book I wrote years earlier about my daughter and I as she would always hide my shoes, trying to get me to stay home. It's sad really. I was so busy with school and work that I missed out on a lot, but at least my parents got to spend time with her. Well, back to that book. I decided to pull it out of the desk drawer and send it off, figured I had nothing to lose, so why not try to get it published.

Well now, I have three different children's book lines. Now this is how I know God has a sense of humor—I am a dyslexic author (laughing). Well, we all need superheroes, and editors are mine.

Now my parents gave me all the "told ya sos" they could as they had told me to do something with that book for so long. But remember, I could color one page, and it was beautiful to them.

Now I had to work and still work on forgiveness. The hardest part of forgiveness for me was knowing that regardless if I ever forgave the exes and life events, the hardest part was knowing that if they or he asked God for forgiveness, they or he would be forgiven. That was a hard one to deal with, but I finally understood. Who was I to judge or hold such authority on anyone? As I know, I am not perfect. So letting it go, focusing more on the power of life, happiness, and using such hard times or evil for good instead of giving so much life to feeding the beast.

Life changed for me. I walked slower. I took time to listen to others, now not just nodding my head but truly listening. I had lost that some time ago. Life is so beautiful you just have to choose to see that way regardless of your life events.

I started talking with my mom more than I ever had before, or I guess I gave her the chance I never really gave her before. She is beautiful still today as she brushed my hair away from my face when she cared for me after my heart procedure. I never told her I was sorry for never giving her a chance, but I was happy I could now realize that her issues were not mine to bear as I had two loving parents with me going through a hard time themselves.

꙳ ꙳

Okay, let's take a seat at the pond for a while if you don't mind. Look at the way the sun hits the water, isn't it beautiful?

Okay, so this whole dating thing was for the birds. At the time, it felt more like a submission of a résumé or you were at an interview. Now I didn't get out too much as I worked a lot and tried focus on the kids. So yes, I went into the online dating game. Wow, what an adventure that was! It felt like a counseling session sometimes as I just have that look about me, "Tell me your problems." Really, those guys just needed someone to talk to as they figured things out for themselves.

The funniest thing to me, looking back on it all, guys would say they were looking for a strong independent woman, then when you're that strong independent woman, they get scared of you.

Well anyway, there are some funny stories I will leave for another time. I gave up on the online dating until a gal I always chatted with at the gas station was so excited to tell she was engaged! I asked her how they met, and she said online. I went and said I tried that, I gave up. She said to just give it one more try. I said, "Okay, fine, I will."

I just put up some picture and didn't fill out any of the little surveys and wrote a little about me. I wasn't going to try to hard. Well, one day, I was clicking through the lineup of photos and going blah, blah, blah at what the guys were saying as I heard it all before. But then I saw this picture of a man, like a manly man, with a beard and soft eyes. He got my attention with his caption, "just a country boy" or something like that. He wasn't trying to be clever. He wrote that he loved his kids, Mother Nature, and worked hard. Well now, this is refreshing. So I decided to write him.

❧ ☙

Let's take this path back if you don't mind. Look at the sunflowers along the fence line.

Okay, well, his first response to me was, "Well hello, darling, I think you're a little out of my league." I fired back not to judge a book by its cover. He replied with, "Good point," and then dating site messages graduated to text messages then calls leading up to our first date (he had me hooked at "darling" just so you know).

We met at the local gun club. We both got out of our vehicles to say hello. I went for the hand shake, and he went for a hug after he took hold of my hand. He invited me over for a walk on his property, and he made me supper. So against every rule I had, I said, "Sure," as I followed him home then up his long driveway and entered his woods. It was so beautiful, but I remember telling myself that this will either be the best thing I have ever done or the worst as I was meeting him in person for the first time at his house out in the middle of the woods. But I did not feel scared, and well, I was just going go with it. It turns out it was the best thing I ever did.

We went for a walk, kind of like this, and just shared about our hopes and dreams or life views and just listened to each other. Then he cooked me one of my favorites, a BLT sandwich with extra tomatoes.

Then we kept talking into the night. Now I don't think I ever laughed so much in my life. I was just me, not trying to be anything but myself as he did the same.

Well, from the moment we first started talking, we have never been apart again. See there over those cattails on the other side of the pond, we were married right there. He made me his wife, and oh, that kiss… well, it was beautiful.

The things he has taught me about life and truly living as me was more than I have ever learned in any classroom. He makes me laugh, he actually pays attention to me, knows when I'm taking life too seriously. He reminds me that life is fun. We are so different in such perfect ways.

He has taught me to care for cattle, mend a fence, how to live with the land in the spirit of Mother Nature. He shared with me so many dreams he had and things he would love to do someday—get back to living with the land and sharing those skills with all of our children.

Well, now my consulting has started to wind down. I had one more heart procedure; that was a month before we got married, and it was time to change direction as I needed a break from social work.

Let's take a seat here for a moment please.

My husband and I were sitting right here watching all the children play. The boys were headed off into the woods to play army, and I said, "Honey, I have an idea." I shared with him a vision of his dreams and mine in a place we call Hick's Place where people can reconnect with Mother Nature and each other in a unique way.

Well, if you look around, that's where we are; there is Hick himself (that's my husband's nickname) doing chores, there is my dad waving at guests arriving, waiting for their outdoor adventure. Look at those smiles of wonder as our guests pile out of their cars.

Well, here we are, right where we started, but it all looks so different now, doesn't it? Look how green the grass is, how bright the flowers are. Oh, listen to the birds sing to us as the children's laughter fills the air.

I work with my dad almost daily. My mom helps when she can as she is off doing things for herself now. My sissy comes and helps when she can, and my bubba stops by when we have big events to help. My husband's parents gave us their blessing to give Hick's Place a try as it's his family's land. You know, I never

CPSIA information can be obtained
at www.ICGtesting.com
Printed in the USA
LVOW04s2055120816
500060LV00016B/200/P

9 781682 070468